ANCIENT CIVILIZATIONS

ANCIENT
INDIA

BY REBECCA ROWELL

Essential Library

An Imprint of Abdo Publishing | www.abdopublishing.com

ANCIENT INDIA

BY REBECCA ROWELL

CONTENT CONSULTANT

Kathleen D. Morrison
Neukom Family Professor and Director
South Asia Language and Area Center
University of Chicago

www.abdopublishing.com

Published by Abdo Publishing, a division of ABDO, PO Box 398166, Minneapolis, Minnesota 55439. Copyright © 2015 by Abdo Consulting Group, Inc. International copyrights reserved in all countries. No part of this book may be reproduced in any form without written permission from the publisher. Essential Library™ is a trademark and logo of Abdo Publishing.

Printed in the United States of America, North Mankato, Minnesota

102014
012015

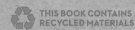
THIS BOOK CONTAINS
RECYCLED MATERIALS

Cover Photos: Corbis, foreground; Rafal Cichawa/Shutterstock Images, background

Interior Photos: Rafal Cichawa/Shutterstock Images, 3; Thinkstock, 6–7; Tatiana Belova/Thinkstock, 8; Shutterstock Images, 10; iStock/Thinkstock, 14; iStockphoto, 16–17, 31, 37, 47, 61, 64–65, 90–91; Omer Saleem/Newscom, 19; National Museum of India, New Delhi, India/Bridgeman Images, 21, 63; North Wind Picture Archives, 24, 93; MCLA Collection/Alamy, 27, 39; Diego Lezama Orezzoli/Corbis, 28–29; Red Line Editorial, 32; Corbis, 40–41; Universal Images Group/SuperStock, 42; Dorling Kindersley/ Thinkstock, 44; Russell Barnett/DK Images, 50; Age Fotostock/SuperStock, 52–53, 78; Dinodia Photos/ Alamy, 55; De Agostini Picture Library/Bridgeman Images, 67; Photos.com/Thinkstock, 74–75; Altaf Qadri/AP Images, 81; Sergio/DK Images, 82–83; Rob Francis/Alamy, 88; Mike Watson Images/ Thinkstock, 96

Editor: Lauren Coss
Series Designer: Jake Nordby

Library of Congress Control Number: 2014943853

Cataloging-in-Publication Data

Rowell, Rebecca.
  Ancient India / Rebecca Rowell.
    p. cm. -- (Ancient civilizations)
  ISBN 978-1-62403-539-5 (lib. bdg.)
  Includes bibliographical references and index.
  1. Indus River Valley--Civilization--Juvenile literature. 2. India--History--Juvenile literature. 3. India-- Social life and customs--Juvenile literature.   I. Title.
  934--dc23

                                                          2014943853

CONTENTS

CHAPTER 1

THE BIRTH OF BUDDHISM

Siddhartha Gautama seemed to have everything anyone could possibly need. His father was King Suddhodana, a member of ancient India's warrior class. Siddhartha lived in approximately the 500s BCE in Kapilavastu, located at the foot of the Himalayan Mountains in an area that is now Nepal.

Siddhartha Gautama, later known as the Buddha, founded Buddhism and was a pivotal figure in ancient Indian history.

The king wanted to protect his son from the woes of the world. Siddhartha grew up in a lavish palace and had everything he could possibly need or want. The king kept Siddhartha from learning about the troubles of life. He did not introduce Siddhartha to religion. The king married Siddhartha to a cousin at age 16. Siddhartha led a mostly secluded life. That changed in his late 20s.

One day, the young man traveled beyond his palace walls for the first time. He saw a sick man. The young prince had never seen a sick person before and asked his chariot driver about the man. The driver explained that everyone gets sick. Intrigued by

Early Buddhism avoided using images of the Buddha, but later followers across Asia created artwork depicting the Buddha.

what he had seen, the prince made three more trips to the world beyond his palace walls. Each time, he saw more scenes of suffering. He also saw death. These scenes were foreign to Siddhartha. His chariot driver explained that people get old and everyone faces death. Siddhartha realized this was his fate, too. Siddhartha also saw an ascetic, someone who lived very simply and strictly, avoiding physical pleasure in an attempt to achieve spiritual enlightenment. The chariot driver told Siddhartha the ascetic had given up the physical pleasures of the world, including food, possessions, and physical contact, in an effort to overcome the fear of suffering and death that humans often experience.

What Siddhartha experienced on his trips beyond his life of comfort affected him greatly. Siddhartha chose to adopt the ascetic lifestyle. At age 29, the young prince walked away from his father, his beautiful home, and his wife and their son. Siddhartha explained the drastic change: "I had been wounded by the enjoyment of the world, and I had come out longing to obtain peace."[1]

"There are countless stories of the Buddha. Each tradition, each culture, each time period has their own stories. We have lots of visual narratives and artwork from all over Buddhist Asia. But the first written material actually, the first biography say of the Buddha really we don't see that before about 500 years after his death. For the first few centuries, Buddhist narrative was oral."[2]

—D. Max Moerman, Buddha scholar

9

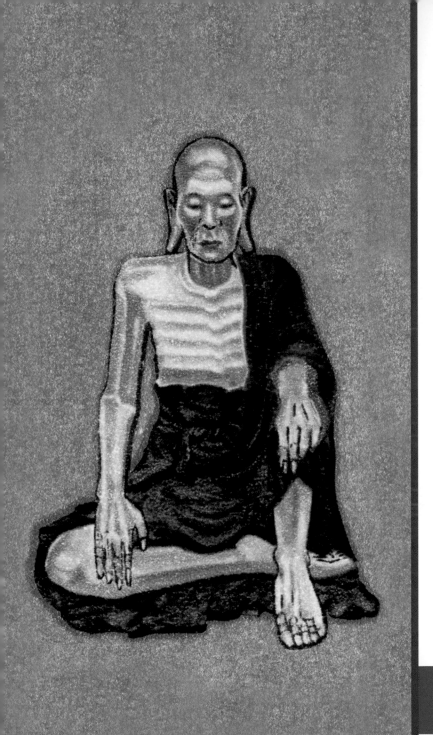

For six years, Siddhartha dedicated himself to his new life. He studied with religious teachers. He practiced yoga. He meditated. Still, Siddhartha did not reach the enlightenment he desired. He joined five ascetics who practiced an extreme form of asceticism. The ascetics believed punishing themselves physically would give them peace and wisdom. Siddhartha lived without shelter, choosing instead to live in the elements. He sat in the cold and in the rain, spending his waking hours meditating. He ate almost nothing. The five men were so impressed by Siddhartha's devotion to his new way of life they became his disciples, or followers. Siddhartha, however, was still not satisfied.

Siddhartha nearly killed himself with his extreme form of asceticism, as shown in a modern artist's interpretation.

Siddhartha's asceticism grew so extreme he ate as little as a single pea a day. One day, a girl offered Siddhartha a bowl of rice. When he agreed to take it, Siddhartha had an important realization: the physical harshness of asceticism was not the way to reach the spiritual goal he desired. He needed to embrace life, and by taking the rice, he did just that.

Siddhartha's five followers thought he had given up on living an ascetic life and stopped following him. They believed he had chosen extravagance over simplicity. However, Siddhartha had not given up his quest. He realized he needed to turn his journey inward.

BECOMING BUDDHA

Siddhartha bathed in a river and then took shelter beneath the Bodhi tree, a sacred fig tree. He decided he would not leave the spot until he achieved enlightenment. He meditated. He saw his current life and previous lives. Siddhartha considered the entire universe. At last, answers emerged to the many questions about suffering he had spent years asking.

Reincarnation

Buddhists believe in *samsara*, or transmigration, which many people call reincarnation. The belief comes from Hinduism. Buddhists and Hindus believe the soul lives on after death and takes on the form of another body. Samsara is the cycle of birth, life, death, and rebirth. The soul continues to be reborn, with each birth affected by the soul's karma, or good or bad conduct in the previous life. When the soul achieves nirvana, or salvation, it has no desires and has achieved a state of passivity. Nirvana releases the soul from samsara. The state of nirvana is eternal, endless, and free of karma.

The Buddha's First Sermon

In his enlightenment, the Buddha realized his early life of luxury and his recent life of asceticism were not the answer to suffering. They were extremes. Enlightenment would come from living a lifestyle between the two, pursuing the middle way. He explained, "There are two ends not to be served by a wanderer. . . . The pursuit of desires and of the pleasure which springs from desire . . . and the pursuit of pain and hardship. The Middle Way . . . avoids both these ends. It is enlightened, it brings clear vision, it makes for wisdom, and leads to peace, insight, enlightenment, and Nirvana."[3]

By morning, Siddhartha had a moment of pure enlightenment. He freed himself from the sufferings all humans faced and gained a new understanding of the universe. At that moment, Siddhartha became the Buddha, the awakened one.

The Buddha, now 35 years old, began teaching. Initially, he was hesitant. He knew it would be difficult to explain what he now understood. Still, he set out, walking more than 100 miles (160 km) before encountering the five ascetics who had once been his followers. In a deer park near Sarnath, which is near the Ganges River in India, the Buddha spoke to them, giving his first lesson. He shared what had happened to him.

The Buddha taught about suffering in principles known as the Four Noble Truths, which address what suffering is, its origin, its end, and the path to its end. The fourth Noble Truth, *Magga*, includes eight steps to ending suffering. The steps address conduct, meditation, and wisdom. Collectively, the steps make up the Eightfold Path, and this path is the middle way the Buddha encouraged, avoiding the extremes of excess and denial. The Four Noble Truths and the Eightfold Path became the foundation of Buddhism, a new religion based on the Buddha's teachings.

THE BUDDHA'S DEATH

For the next 45 years, the Buddha traveled and taught. At age 80, he accepted a meal of spoiled food. The food made him sick. He lay down in Kushinagar, in northeast India, and died.

Before dying, the awakened one told his followers to continue their Buddhist work. He spoke of dharma, Buddhism's basic principle for existence:

It may be that after I am gone that some of you will think, "now we have no teacher." But that is not how you should see it. Let the Dharma and the discipline that I have taught you be your teacher. All individual things pass away. Strive on, untiringly.[4]

INVALUABLE CONTRIBUTIONS

The Buddha's teachings eventually spread around the world. Buddhism still has many followers today.

The Buddha's Monks

The Buddha had disciples. They formed the *sangha*, the Buddhist monastic community. Initially, Buddhist monks were only men. Toward the end of his life, the Buddha agreed to allow women to join the sangha. Disciples who achieved enlightenment were known as *arahants*, or noble ones.

Four Holy Sites

Buddhism has four holy sites. Lumpini, near Kapilavastu, Nepal, is where the Buddha was born as Siddhartha Gautama. Bodh Gaya, in northeast India, is where Siddhartha gained enlightenment while sitting beneath the Bodhi tree and became the Buddha. Sarnath, in northeast India, is where the Buddha gave his first lecture. Kushinagar, in northeast India, is where the Buddha died. All four sites include structures that Ashoka, a Buddhist whom many historians consider to be India's greatest emperor, built during his reign in the 200s BCE.

However, Buddhism is only one of the religions that emerged from ancient India. Three major religions coexisted during this time. Jainism started at approximately the same time as Buddhism. And both Jainism and Buddhism were reactions to a form of Hinduism that had begun in India generations earlier.

India is home to some of the oldest civilizations on Earth. By the time the Buddha was born, people had inhabited the area for thousands of years. They were drawn to India's rivers as early as prehistoric times. Once there, people began settling down, taking advantage of the rich soil to establish farms. Over time, settlements became cities, governments formed, and economies developed. Kings ruled and empires came and went, destroyed and built anew by domestic and foreign attackers. All the while, a rich culture developed and matured.

Ancient India's contributions to the world are far more than religious. People of the subcontinent developed great literature and art. They created yoga and medical practices that are still popular today. Ancient Indians also made significant contributions to science. The mathematics individuals, businesses, and machines use every day is possible because of Indian discoveries. From its words to its numbers—and long before, with its first settlements—ancient India helped form the world as we know it today.

ANCIENT INDIA, CIRCA 200 BCE

N

CHAPTER 2

SETTLING THE SUBCONTINENT

The Indus, or Harappan, people stand out in India's history. Their existence makes ancient India a unique place. Their time exhibited great growth and achievements, including the development of major urban centers. More than 3,000 years before the birth of Jesus, the people of the Indus settled in South Asia,

The Indus River played an important role in the earliest Indian civilizations, as well as more recent ones.

establishing what would become one of the world's first civilizations and the foundation of the rich Indian culture that thrives today.

THE INDUS CIVILIZATION

The Indus civilization takes its name from the Indus River, one of the major rivers that runs through the region where the Indus people settled, an area that is now Pakistan and northwest India. The earliest Indus people settled in 3300 BCE. The high point of the civilization was from approximately 2600 BCE to 1700 BCE. During that time, the Indus people developed a variety of settlements. The largest settlement that has been excavated is

Bhimbetka's Prehistoric Inhabitants

People have occupied the subcontinent of India for hundreds of thousands of years. Archaeological finds place prehumans in India 500,000 years ago. Modern humans probably arrived in India between 70,000 and 60,000 years ago. Over time, communities developed, including Bhimbetka, in central India. There, approximately 10,000 years ago, people left their mark on rock shelters. Their artwork is the earliest known in India and provides a glimpse into life at that time. The prehistoric artists used paint made from animal fat, colored earth, roots, and vegetable dyes. Their brushes were made from stringy branches.

Paintings show a variety of animals, including bison, deer, elephants, a peacock, and a snake. The art also features hunters carrying weapons such as bows and arrows. Some hunters carry swords and shields. One scene details a hunter running from a bison.

Tourists can still visit the ancient city of Mohenjo-Daro, now part of Pakistan.

Mohenjo-Daro. Harappa was another major Indus city, with a population of roughly 30,000.[1] The two cities were approximately 400 miles (640 km) apart.[2] Each city occupied roughly one square mile (2.6 sq km).[3]

Harappa's and Mohenjo-Daro's designs were quite complex. The cities were laid out in a rectangle. Features included wide roads, large homes, citadels, and granaries. Canals allowed for irrigation. A drainage system of sewers lined with bricks was likely the first sanitation system in the world.

The Indus civilization included hundreds more sites. It stretched hundreds of miles in every direction, making it the largest of the world's earliest known civilizations, bigger than Egypt and Mesopotamia.

A CLOSER LOOK

INDUS SEALS

Sir John Marshall, a British archaeologist, headed the Indian Archaeological Survey from 1902 to 1931. He oversaw digs at Harappa and Mohenjo-Daro, unearthing similar clay seals at both locations. The Indus people used them in trading, stamping a seal's image on pottery or on clay tags.

Marshall learned a similar seal existed in the Middle East, in Mesopotamia (modern Iraq). Archaeologists dated that seal to approximately 2300 BCE, which provided a date for the Indian discoveries. The similarities between the seals also connected the people in India and Mesopotamia via trade.

Archaeologists have since recovered thousands of seals. Several are square, measuring approximately 0.75 inch by 0.75 inch (1.9 cm by 1.9 cm).[4] They are made of soapstone. The seals feature a variety of figures, including gods and animals such as bulls and elephants. The unicorn often appears on seals. Seals often include writing. Scholars have not yet deciphered the system of symbols the Indus people used.

By approximately 1900 BCE, cities in the Indus Valley began declining. Scholars have different opinions as to why. Possible reasons include flooding and climate changes, which would have affected farming and may have led to economic hardship.

THE VEDIC AGE

The Vedic civilization succeeded the Indus, lasting from 1700 BCE to 500 BCE. The word *Vedic* comes from the *Vedas*, which are the texts of the Hindu religion written during this time. The beginning of the Vedic period is marked by a group of people migrating onto the subcontinent who called

Indus Settlement Hierarchy

Archaeologists have discovered remains of the Indus civilization between the Indus and Ganges Rivers and well beyond, and they have categorized settlements into four tiers by size.[5]

Tier	Size	Characteristics	Quantity
1	200 to 250 acres (80 to 100 ha)	These sites had similar architecture, including walled enclosures.	5
2	Approximately 50 acres (20 ha)	These sites have features similar to the larger tier 1 sites.	32
3	Average 7.5 acres (3 ha)	These smaller sites had fortifications.	More than 32
4	2.5 acres (1 ha)	These locations were villages or centers for a particular craft.	Almost 15,000

themselves *Arya*, "the noble ones." They arrived in approximately 1500 BCE. The Arya were a semi-nomadic people who spoke Indo-Aryan languages. Their origin is not quite certain. Scholars have hypothesized the group came from Central Asia, Iran, Russia, and Scandinavia.

During this time, many different groups called ancient India home. Some were nomads, others farmed, and others lived in villages and large towns. The Indo-Aryan speakers lived an agriculture-based lifestyle for the most part, and they spread out across the subcontinent, intermixing with the people already living there. They occupied land stretching west from the Punjab, the region of the Indus River and its tributaries, to the Ganges River. The Vedic civilization formed the foundation of Hinduism and of modern Indian culture, including the caste system, which divided the population into distinct social classes.

During the latter part of the Vedic age, in 600 BCE, 16 *mahajanapadas*, "great kingdoms," emerged. This time would also bring about great changes in ancient India's religious beliefs with the birth of two religious leaders. Mahavira, born in 599 BCE, would found Jainism. Siddhartha Gautama, born in approximately the 500s BCE, became the Buddha and founded Buddhism. Neither man believed in Hinduism, the prevailing religion of the Vedic civilization, and each formed his own set of beliefs to counter it.

King Porus surrendered to Alexander the Great after losing the Battle of Hydaspes.

ALEXANDER THE GREAT

Less than a century after the mahajanapadas began, the ancient Indians found themselves fighting invaders from Persia and then Greece. Greek traders had long been visiting ports along India's coasts. Then, in the 300s BCE, the Greeks attacked under the direction of skilled leader

Alexander III. He was a Greek king known as Alexander the Great for his military achievements. In 327 BCE, he became the first Greek to invade India. Alexander took over Taxila and Aornos, two cities in the north. Next, he challenged Porus, an Indian king, in 326 BCE in the Battle of Hydaspes. After defeating Porus, Alexander led his troops to victory along the Indus River. Once Alexander and his men reached the mouth of the Indus, they headed back westward, toward their homeland.

While in India, Alexander established many Greek communities. These aided Indian communication and trade with the Greek empire. However,

India's Name

India's name reflects its geography. The region's early settlers called the area *sindhu*, a word that means "river frontier" in Sanskrit, a language that developed in ancient India during the Vedic period. The name came from the many rivers that ran through the region. In fact, today's Punjab Province was once called *Sapta-Sindhava*, "land of seven rivers." The *Rigveda*, an ancient sacred book, discusses the area. Five of the rivers still exist: the Chenab, Indus, Jhelum, Ravi, and Sutlej/Beas. The other two rivers, the Drasadvati and Saraswati, dried up long ago.

Persians used a different word when they began exploring ancient India in the 500s BCE. They called the Indus River and the people who lived near it *Hindhu*, a variation of *sindhu*. The Greeks introduced the word *India*. When Alexander the Great invaded in the 300s BCE, he and his army called the river *Indos* and the area around it *India*.

Alexander wanted the communities to do more. Alexander wanted to unite Asia and Europe into a single country. He supported marriage between Indians and Greeks, and he encouraged the spread of Greek customs in India, as well as the rest of his empire. Alexander's grand plan would not come to life. He died suddenly in 323 BCE, and his great empire was gone in little more than ten years. However, a new Indian empire was on the rise.

GREAT EMPIRES

Only two years after Alexander's invasion, India's first empire began. In 321 BCE, Chandragupta Maurya founded the Mauryan Empire, uniting almost the entire Indian subcontinent. Chandragupta expanded his empire by invading neighboring lands, including areas Alexander had captured in modern-day Afghanistan. Chandragupta created a strong government that led to a strong economy.

The Mauryan Empire Chandragupta founded would last more than 130 years, ending in 185 BCE. Before its decline, the empire would have a leader even greater than its founder. Ashoka, Chandragupta's grandson, was a powerful leader who spread Buddhism across the subcontinent. Ashoka became one of India's most celebrated emperors.

After a series of invasions and different dynasties, India's next great empire emerged in 320 CE. Its founder was Chandragupta I, a chief in the

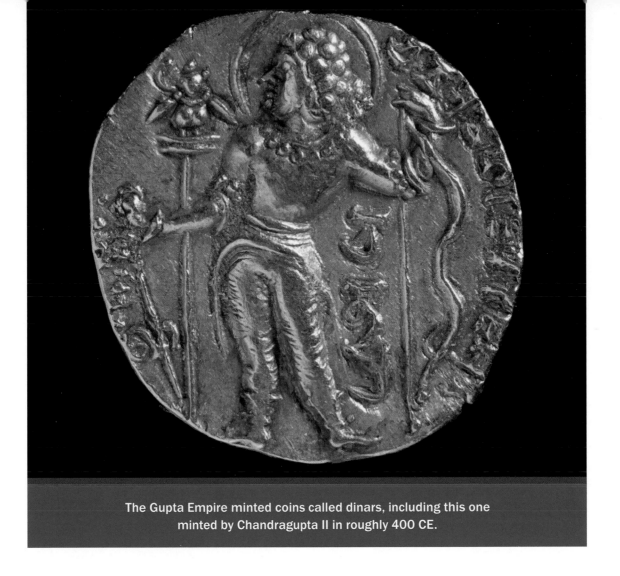

The Gupta Empire minted coins called dinars, including this one minted by Chandragupta II in roughly 400 CE.

Magadha kingdom. Marriage made him leader of the Ganges Valley. He joined the two territories into his own empire. The Gupta Empire would last until 550 CE. Its leaders, the Guptas, oversaw an era of great cultural achievement and economic success.

CHAPTER 3

CHIEFS, KINGS, AND CASTES

Government and economics in ancient India, like its different civilizations, developed with time. As the nomadic groups settled, they organized and leaders emerged. Little is known about the governments of India's earliest civilization, the Indus. However, the organization and complexity of cities such as those uncovered at Harappa and

The complex layout of Mohenjo-Daro took careful planning that suggests an organized government.

Mohenjo-Daro suggest some sort of government existed. Leaders likely focused on securing the food supply, needing vast supplies to feed the large population. Fortunately, Mohenjo-Daro had sufficient supplies, buying food from nearby farmers and fisherman.

Archaeologists studying the sites have found no evidence of a king or queen. Instead of a single leader who controlled the wealth, the government seems to have focused on sharing the resources of the society and its people.

The Indus economy was largely agricultural. Livestock included cattle, goats, and sheep. The main crops were barley and wheat. Trade was strong at the end of the Indus period. Evidence suggests trading with several far-flung regions, including Mesopotamia and other parts of the Middle East. Indus traders exchanged textiles and items such as beads and dice for resources such as lapis lazuli gemstones and tin.

FROM CHIEFS TO A KING

During the Vedic era, the city life of the Indus civilization gave way to a more rustic life as the Indo-Aryans focused on raising cattle. Later, they transitioned to agriculture, cutting down trees in the forest around the Ganges River to farm the land. The *Rigveda*, a sacred ancient Indian book, discusses the agricultural lifestyle, including how farmers used plows and

Barley is still grown in India today.

harvested grain. Many Indo-Aryans settled in *janas*, small tribal groups. Each jana had a *rajan*, "chief," and *samiti* and a *sabha*, which were ruling councils. The janas frequently fought one another, battling for property and livestock.

By 800 BCE, the janas had grown into clearly marked *janapadas*, small kingdoms led by a *raja*, or king. The raja relied on two people. The *senani* led the army. The *purohita* was a priest who acted like a shaman or medicine man by treating illnesses with spells. Tribes soon grew to become mahajanapadas. Power shifted from the countryside to urban areas.

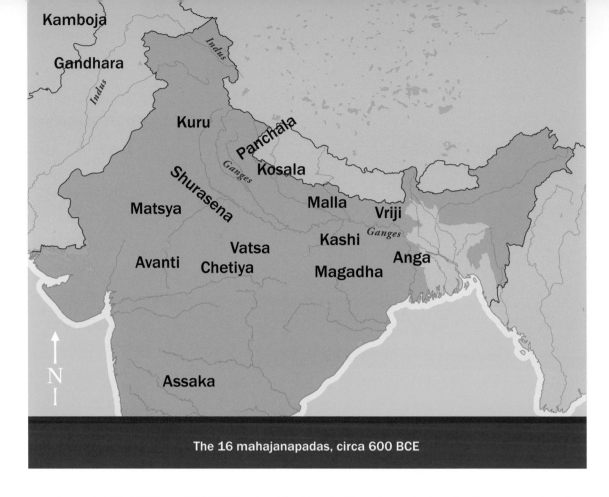

The 16 mahajanapadas, circa 600 BCE

From 1000 BCE to 600 BCE, the Vedic civilization thrived. The growth of settlements created additional jobs. In addition to raising cattle and farming, the Indo-Aryans worked as carpenters, goldsmiths, potters, and tanners. They made bows and chariots.

By 600 BCE, India had 16 mahajanapadas. Magadha became the most powerful of these. However, other forms of government existed as well.

Several small republics stood alongside the mahajanapadas. Kings ruled the republics, but their governments also had elements of democracy, including executive, judicial, and legislative branches. As supreme leader, the king had final say in the decisions of all branches. He also appointed the officials who held positions in the kingdom's administration.

THE MAURYAN PERIOD

A major shift in government highlighted the period following the Vedic era. In 321 BCE, when Chandragupta Maurya united India's many kingdoms into an empire spanning nearly the entire subcontinent, he also created a central government. It was located in Pataliputra, the empire's capital. Chandragupta's system of government consisted of levels. The smallest was the village, each with a headman and a council serving as a local government. The next level was the district, which consisted of groups of villages. Provinces consisted of groups of districts. Governors were the government representatives at the province level.

This strengthening of government structure helped the economy. The Mauryan Empire had a strong and active trade—internally and externally. International trading partners included Persia and Greece. Agriculture blossomed. The booming economy included currency. Chandragupta's thriving empire minted and used silver coins.

In approximately 297 BCE, Chandragupta gave up his position. His son, Bindusura, became emperor. Bindusura expanded and strengthened the empire. Between 273 and 268 BCE, he passed on the empire to his own son, Ashoka, who would prove even more successful.

A skilled military leader, Ashoka extended the Mauryan Empire even farther. His victories included defeating the country of Kalinga, which today is part of the northeastern Indian state of Orissa, in the 260s BCE. However, the bloody battle for Kalinga changed Ashoka. He was troubled by the pain he and his army caused. They had killed thousands in their conquest of Kalinga. He gave up fighting and converted to Buddhism.

Kautilya and *Artha-Shastra*

Much of Chandragupta Maurya's success was due to his adviser Kautilya. Kautilya helped Chandragupta overthrow the Nanda dynasty and gain control of the Magadha region, which led to Chandragupta establishing an empire. Kautilya also wrote *Artha-Shastra*, or *The Science of Material Gain*, a book Chandragupta relied on to guide his rule. The text has 15 chapters, each of which addresses a facet of government. In his book, Kautilya promotes the use of assassination and spies. Although some have judged Kautilya negatively for some of the activities he recommended, he possessed great knowledge of human behavior and politics. Many historians believe Kautilya was indispensible for the Mauryan Empire to achieve its greatness.

Ashoka shared his newfound beliefs in a number of edicts, which were carved in locations throughout the kingdom and intended to inspire his people. He shares his compassion in one of them:

All men are my children. As for my own children, I desire that they may be provided with all the welfare and happiness of this world and of the next, so do I desire for all men as well.[1]

Ashoka's governing reflected his faith. He changed laws made by his father and grandfather, making legislation less harsh. He banned forced labor. And he restricted the killing of animals by prohibiting hunting and limiting slaughter to only what was necessary. External efforts included strengthening connections with Asian and European countries. The Buddhist emperor was a successful leader, and the Mauryan Empire during Ashoka's reign was peaceful, stable, and prosperous. The emperor's devotion to his beliefs made their mark on India's history, which has come to know him as Ashoka the Great.

THE GUPTAS

Following Ashoka's death in 232 BCE, the Mauryan Empire declined. The end of the empire brought a succession of dynasties. With each century, India moved away from the unified glory of its time under Ashoka's thoughtful rule. That changed with the emergence of the Gupta Empire in 320 CE.

A CLOSER LOOK

ASHOKA LEAVES HIS MARK

Ashoka had more than 30 edicts carved throughout the kingdom in caves and on rocks and stone pillars. In these proclamations, he shared rules for living that were moral and based on the dharma. Ashoka strived to spread Buddhism, and many edicts relate to Buddhist principles. In addition to sharing his beliefs through edicts, Ashoka ordered the construction of many monasteries and stupas, a type of shrine. He also held a Buddhist council at Pataliputra, Maurya's capital. Ashoka believed so strongly in his adopted faith he sent Mahindra and Sanghamitra, his twin son and daughter, to Sri Lanka to spread Buddhism.

The Great Stupa at Sanchi in the modern Indian state of Uttar Pradesh stands among a complex of related Buddhist sites. Tradition says a portion of the Buddha's remains was buried here, along with those of another disciple. The current stupa is an enlargement of Ashoka's older construction. Its large dome is richly decorated with carvings representing the Buddha's life.

Chandragupta I was a local chief in the Magadha kingdom. His power grew when he married the princess of a tribe controlling much of northeastern India, which added the Ganges Valley to his realm.

Samudragupta succeeded his father, Chandragupta I. Like Ashoka, Samudragupta was a great military man. During his reign, he expanded the empire through many battles. He established the capital of his empire in Pataliputra, just as Chandragupta Maurya, founder of the Mauryan Empire had done several centuries earlier. However, the emperor was interested in more than fighting. He enjoyed music and poetry, and he was skilled at both. Samudragupta was a Hindu, but he tolerated other religions.

The Gupta Empire continued growing after Samudragupta's death in 380 CE. Chandragupta II took power, and he would prove to be the most successful of the Guptas. He continued expanding the Gupta Empire, relying on military action and arranged marriages between his children and those of other leaders to extend his reach and power. This helped him gain control over trade routes, which strengthened the economy. And the economy was good. The empire minted gold coins with images of the Guptas.

Chandragupta II's government was strong and included a second capital at Ujjain. The Guptas supported cultural development, including the arts, education, and medicine. They sought to improve the lives of their people,

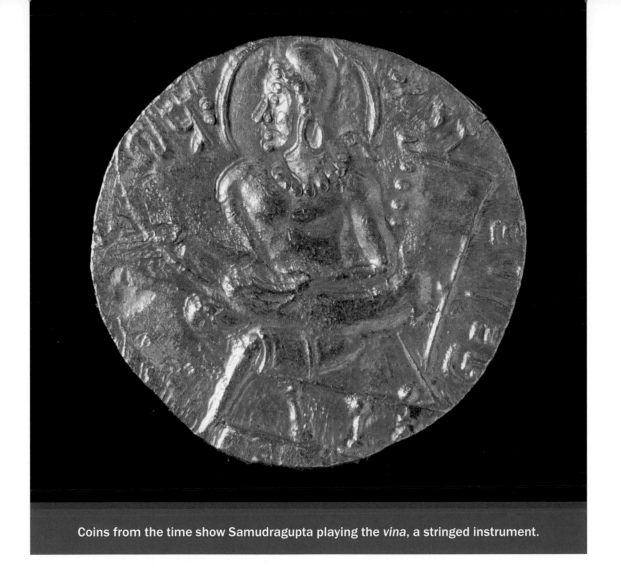

Coins from the time show Samudragupta playing the *vina*, a stringed instrument.

building free hospitals, monasteries, and universities. Culture flourished in the Gupta Empire. For this reason, many scholars consider the Gupta era to be a golden age of India's history.

CHAPTER 4

LIFE BASED IN FAITH

Daily life in ancient India was like modern life in many mays. People had relationships, they honored rituals and customs, and they survived by creating homes and finding meals. Depending on who was governing, life was easier during some eras than in others.

Sculptures, such as this one uncovered at Mohenjo-Daro, help historians understand the importance of agriculture in ancient India.

MEN, WOMEN, AND THE CASTE SYSTEM

The Indus people appear to have differed from other ancient groups in that women played an important role, at least in religion. Thousands of ceramic sculptures exist that depict women. They often take the form of goddesses, especially mother goddesses, suggesting the society revered females. The generally patriarchal society of the Indo-Aryans suggests they considered women less highly. Fathers headed most families, and the mother answered to the father. Families usually prized sons over daughters.

One important facet of relationships in ancient India involved the caste system. Ancient Indian society

Archaeologists have discovered several mother goddess sculptures in Mohenjo-Daro.

consisted of three major groups: priests, rulers, and producers. During the Vedic period, the Indo-Aryans introduced the caste system, which was similar and split society into four main *varnas*, "classes," based on occupation. The Brahmin, "priest," varna was the highest and most powerful caste. The Kshatriya, "noble," was the second varna and consisted of those who ruled and fought. Merchants and traders belonged to the third varna: Vaishya, "commoner." Members of the lowest class, the Shudra, "servant," were workers.

With time, the castes became more rigid socially. By the 200s BCE, the castes had changed to being hereditary rather than determined by occupation, meaning people were born into them. The castes affected several aspects of life. For one, members of different castes were not allowed to marry one another. Members of a caste could take an offering of food from someone in a higher caste but not from someone in a lower caste. In addition, access to temples also varied by caste. Brahmins had complete access and led religious activities. The Kshatriya and Vaishya were allowed to worship, but sometimes the Shudra were prevented from making sacrifices.

FOOD AND COOKING

The peoples of ancient India ate a varied diet. Initially, grain was a cornerstone. Rice has been around for thousands of years. By approximately

400 BCE, rice was a key crop in northern India. The Indo-Aryans ate a lot of rice, sometimes boiled. It was also eaten with milk and curd, or yogurt. Millets and pulses, a branch of the legume family that includes lentils and peas, were eaten throughout the subcontinent.

As foods changed, grain remained a key crop. Barley—especially fried barley—appears regularly in the *Rigveda*. *Saktu*, or pulverized grain, was also common. Cuisine also included crushed grain combined with curd. *Puroddsa* was a type of cake people during the Vedic era used as part of rituals, in which they also sacrificed animals.

Meats from buffalo, bulls, dogs, and horses were sometimes eaten as part of a meal. Later, meat of barren cows and sterile oxen became delicacies, as did meat from goats and sheep. However, the popularity of meat changed with the rise and spread of Jainism and Buddhism, which stressed not harming any living being, including killing and eating animals and fish. Vegetarianism became more common.

Depending on the era and the faith, certain foods were not supposed to be eaten. The *Dharma sutras*, which means "righteousness thread" in Sanskrit, provided the earliest laws for Hindus, including guidelines for

Although ancient India was divided into four castes, the rules during the Vedic period were not as strict as they were later.

eating. Some aquatic animals were prohibited, including the porpoise. A variety of plant items were also not allowed, including garlic, mushrooms, and sprouts.

While many ancient Indians faced certain restrictions, there were plenty of other foods to enjoy. Fruits included dates and mangoes. Honey and sugarcane juice added sweetness to the menu, too. With time, milk products were developed. In addition to curd, people used curdled milk; porridge; cream; a mixture of curd and milk; the thickened surface of milk; butter in various forms; and a mixture of milk, curd, honey, and butter. Many of the spices used today were also part of ancient Indian cooking. Early options included salt, black pepper, and long pepper, a spicier, more flavorful relative of black pepper.

To wash down their meals, the peoples of ancient India enjoyed an assortment of beverages. Wine was popular. *Takra* was a mixture of buttermilk and water. *Mantha* was barley meal mixed in curd, malted butter, milk, or water. *Madhuparka* was a blend of curd, honey, sugar, water, and ghee, a type of butter.

Utensils were made of clay, metal, stone, and wood. Lower classes using metal likely had utensils made of copper and iron, while upper classes may have had gold and silver. Household items included pots, plates, and pitchers. Bags made of leather held various ingredients, ranging from ghee or oil to honey or grains.

CLOTHING

Clay artifacts provide clues to the wardrobe of the Indus people. Terra-cotta figures are adorned in what scholars believe is cotton. Researchers have also uncovered beads containing silk fibers. The *Vedas* mention wool. However, the bulk of researchers' understanding of ancient Indian garb comes from sculptures and paintings in caves.

The artwork shows ancient Indians wearing fabric in different ways, wrapping various parts of the body in a dhoti, sari, or turban. A dhoti is a long piece of fabric worn as a loincloth. Both men and

Many women in India still wear the traditional sari.

women wore the garment, wrapping the length of material around the legs and hips and tucking the ends into material at the waist. The upper bodies for both men and women were often left bare. A sari is also a long piece of fabric. Women wore it wrapped around the body in such a way as to form a skirt with one end of the fabric and a head or shoulder covering with the other.

During the Vedic period, ancient Indians began wearing three pieces of clothing. The *antariya* was white cotton or muslin and went around the waist, held in place by a *kayabandh*, a sash. An *uttariya* was a scarf that covered the torso.

The people in ancient India dyed their fabrics a variety of colors. Indigo, madder red, and safflower, also a red, were common. In addition, the *Vishnudharmottara*, an ancient Hindu text about painting, lists five shades of white: August moon, August clouds after the rain, conch shell, ivory, and jasmine.

HOUSING

Archaeologists have uncovered evidence that the people of ancient India were accomplished at construction. Excavations at Harappa and Mohenjo-Daro have revealed the Indus people were skilled planners and builders. The cities were organized in a grid, with a main street, side streets, and alleys. Archaeologists discovered remains of many buildings, some of which they think were public areas. Many others were likely private houses.

Houses were at least two stories tall and built around a central courtyard into which the rooms of the house opened. The ground floor usually did not have windows, which provided more privacy and helped keep out street noise and thieves. Upper floors had screened windows. The screens were grills made of alabaster, terra-cotta, or wood. The main door was behind the house, on the alley. The rooms of the house lined the courtyard, and a balcony, made of wood, likely looked out over it. People accessed upper floors via a brick stairway.

Many houses had a well. Many also had a toilet. And most houses had a platform for bathing. Builders constructed these ancient indoor conveniences against outside walls. There, water and waste would flow down drains and into a city drainage system. Houses also had chutes for garbage that carried refuse to bins at the ground level.

The Fate of Mohenjo-Daro

In 2014, after existing for approximately 4,500 years, what remains of Mohenjo-Daro was at risk for being lost forever. Dr. Asma Ibrahim, a prominent Pakistani archaeologist, explained, "Every time I come here, I feel worse than the previous time. I haven't been back for two or three years. The losses since then are so immense and it breaks my heart."[1]

Ibrahim was referring to the deterioration caused by humidity, rain, and salt. Efforts to conserve the site were problematic, too. Ibrahim was clear about the severity of the situation, noting, "In my assessment, the site will not last more than 20 years."[2] Some researchers have proposed burying the site again to stop its deterioration.

Through excavations, archaeologists have been able to determine what a typical Mohenjo-Daro house may have looked like.

The Indo-Aryan people who arrived from the north during the Vedic era did not have such sophisticated houses as the Indus civilization. Their housing reflected their nomadic lifestyle and were basic buildings constructed of mud.

WAY OF LIFE

The remains of the houses and other evidence from Harappa and Mohenjo-Daro suggest the Indus people in those cities lived relatively comfortably. In addition to having thoughtfully planned cities and homes, they seemed to have lived in a society of equality. Archaeologists have not found grand palaces or fancy temples—structures that might suggest a class of ruling elite.

While the Indus civilization thrived culturally, its people were civil and law-abiding. Archaeological findings of the period suggest the groups lived peacefully, fighting neither internally nor externally. In addition, crime seems to have been almost nonexistent.

Daily life varied greatly in ancient India. Its richness reflects changing knowledge, beliefs, and ideas by a developing culture. Life in ancient India was based in faith, a tradition that continues today.

CHAPTER 5

LITERATURE, ART, MUSIC, AND DANCE

Ancient India's culture is rich and varied. Foremost is its literature, which has survived for millennia. Other creative endeavors, including art and dance, have also stood the test of time.

Writing on the Kanheri Caves, near Mumbai, India, was inscribed between the 100s BCE and the 900s CE.

LANGUAGE

Artifacts such as seals show the Indus people used a system of symbols for their written language. Researchers have recovered almost 4,200 items with the writing. The characters number in the hundreds and were written from right to left. Most items with symbols are very small. The longest string of characters, 17, appeared on an item measuring only one square inch (6.5 sq cm).[1] No one has deciphered the Indus writing system.

Sanskrit, developed later, holds a prominent position in India's history. It is part of the Indo-European language group, grammatically similar to Greek and Latin, which are part of the same group. Sanskrit is still spoken in India today. In the 400s BCE, grammarian Panini laid out the structure of the language in the *Astadhyayi*, which means "eight chapters." His book defines classical Sanskrit's grammar, including nouns, pronouns, and verbs. Through history, people have written Sanskrit using a variety of systems, with scripts varying by region.

LITERATURE

The peoples of ancient India produced an abundance of literature—most of it written in Sanskrit. Much of it is religious, particularly Hindu. The *Vedas*, an assortment of texts written during the Vedic period, have also provided the world with considerable information about life at that time.

The *Vedas* are still in print in multiple languages and read in India and around the world.

Veda is a Sanskrit word meaning "knowledge." The *Vedas* contain a wealth of material that was initially passed along orally, spoken by one generation to the next. The material is divided into several collections. Much of the content developed from hymns about sacrifice, which honor the Hindu gods the Indo-Aryans worshiped. The *Vedas* address magic as well, providing charms and spells for Indo-Aryan priests.

The first four Vedic texts feature collections of hymns known as the Samhitas. The *Rigveda*, "Knowledge of Verses," is the oldest Vedic Samhita, dating to approximately 1200 BCE. Its ten books contain 1,028 hymns, which cover a variety of topics. "The Waters of Life" acknowledges the importance of water:

Waters, you are the ones who bring us the life force.

Help us to find nourishment so that we may look upon great joy.

Let us share in the most delicious sap that you have, as if you were loving mothers.[2]

The *Yajurveda*, "Knowledge of the Sacrifice," has mantras for a priest to recite when leading a sacrificial ritual. The *Samaveda*, "Knowledge of the Chants," contains verses for chanting. The fourth Samhita, the *Atharvaveda*, "Knowledge of the Fire Priest," has information on magic. All four Samhitas of the *Vedas* address more than religion. Other topics include philosophy, mathematics, medicine, science, and yoga.

Additional Vedic texts came after the first four *Vedas*. The *Brahmanas*, written in approximately 900 BCE, address prayer and rituals for the top members of society. The *Aranyakas*, "Forest Books," followed. These contain understanding that can be obtained only through being alone in a forest.

The *Upanishads*, probably written between 600 BCE and 100 BCE, were the last of the *Vedas* the Indo-Aryans wrote. Topics covered include philosophy, religion, and the origin of the universe.

POETRY

Ancient India's extensive collection of writing includes two great epic poems: the *Ramayana* and the *Mahabharata*. Both are in Sanskrit, and both describe a battle of good versus evil. The *Ramayana*, "Romance of Rama," is the older of the two great poems. It began as an oral story that may date as far back as 1500 BCE. The poet Valmiki wrote down the story sometime after 300 BCE.

The *Ramayana* tells the story of Rama, the seventh incarnation of Vishnu, a popular Hindu god. Through its approximately 24,000 couplets, which are divided among seven books, the *Ramayana* teaches values such as devotion, duty, morality, and valor.

The *Mahabharata*, "Great Epic of the Bharata Dynasty," is considerably longer. Its 18 books contain

Kalidasa

Kalidasa may have been India's most prolific writer. He wrote poetry and dramas in Sanskrit during the 400s CE, during the time of the Guptas. He wrote at least six works: three dramas, two epic poems, and a lyric poem. *Abhijnanashakuntala*, "The Recognition of Shakuntala," is his best-known drama. It explains how King Dushyanta seduced Shakuntala, a nymph, and then rejected her and their child, Bharata. Ultimately, the family is reunited in heaven. Some scholars believe it is the best work of Indian literature of all time.

Dharma

Dharma is an important idea in Hinduism, Buddhism, and Jainism. Its meaning varies among the three religions. In Hinduism, dharma is the religious and moral law that guides behavior. In Buddhism, dharma is the universal truth that all individuals share at all times, especially the ideas of karma and samsara. People have interpreted the word *dharma* in Buddhism many ways, including "law, truth, doctrine, gospel, teaching, norm, and true idea."[4]

In Jainism, dharma is moral virtue. For Jains, dharma is also a substance, an immortal and infinite life force that gives organisms the ability to move.

220,000 lines, which make it the longest poem in the world.[3] Legend attributes its writing to Vyasa, a wise man. Vyasa wrote the great poem approximately 100 years after Valmiki wrote the *Ramayana*.

The *Mahabharata* tells the story of two groups of sons in a royal family as the cousins fight for power. The text is valuable to Hindus and non-Hindus alike. It teaches dharma, or morality. It also provides historical information about the religion, including its development from 400 BCE to 200 CE.

ART AND ARCHITECTURE

Ancient Indians also expressed their beliefs and stories through their visual art. The inhabitants of India have been artists for hundreds of thousands of years. Paintings such as those in Bhimbetka, in central India, date to prehistoric times. People of the Indus civilization worked with clay. They drew figures—human and animal—and symbols into their now famous seals and other earthenware.

The people of ancient India were also sculptors. They modeled simple shapes, such as carts, cattle, and monkeys, with terra-cotta. The female form was popular, too, particularly in Indus art.

As Buddhism became more popular in India, it became the focus of much of India's early art and architecture. Some of Ashoka's edicts were inscribed on pillars adorned with animal shapes. He also had stupas built or restored, honoring his belief in Buddhism by helping preserve remains of the Buddha.

During the second and first centuries BCE, Indian artists honored the Buddha in Ajanta in west-central India. There, they carved caves to serve as temples, adorning them with monuments and paintings of the Buddha's life.

The Buddhist focus continued during the beginning of the new millennium. Artists in the first, second, and third centuries CE concentrated on building more stupas. Their carvings told stories. The style was ornate and more complex.

Later, in the 400s and 500s, during the Gupta period, artists added to Ajanta, creating more caves and artwork. Painters worked almost exclusively on plaster.

A CLOSER LOOK

THE CAVES OF AJANTA

Near India's center, 29 caves serve as a record of the country's artistic development. Artists carved the caves into the Sahyadri Hills in west-central India. Skilled carvers shaped the first caves in the 100s BCE, creating five sanctuaries. The design is similar to that of a basilica, with a long hall and side aisles separated by pillars. Artists decorated the caves with sculptures and paintings depicting the Buddha's life.

Craftsmen added additional caves during the 400s and 500s CE. The additions served as monasteries, becoming home to approximately 200 Buddhist monks and artisans. The people who crafted the newer caves based the design on that of the earlier structures, adding to them. Ajanta's sculptures and paintings are an exceptional example of Buddhist art and mark the start of classical Indian art.

MUSIC

Visual art provides clues to music in ancient India. Statues from the Indus period show instruments such as drums and a bow-shaped harp. Like other art from the time, music during the Vedic era focused on religion, serving two purposes: to please the gods and as part of sacrificial rituals. The *Rigveda* includes spoken hymns. The *Samaveda*, "Knowledge of the Chants," is a Hindu book of songs. Its hymns are chanted, using seven musical notes. Vedic music includes pieces for individuals and groups.

Literature reveals some of music's history, but few specific details are mentioned. The *Ramayana* discusses a lute. The *Mahabharata* details a musical scale with seven notes. And both Buddhist and Jain texts mention singing.

During the Gupta era, in approximately 400 CE, a book of music known as the *Dattilam* was created by the sage Dattila Muni. It describes a system for music that includes notes and how to arrange them.

DANCE

Like other forms of expression, dance often related closely to religion. Dance in ancient India dates back at least 4,500 years. Artwork and Vedic literature, including the *Mahabharata*, mentions dance. Ancient Indian dance was a form of worship. It reflected *rasa*, which are nine emotions: anger, compassion, courage, disgust, fear, happiness, serenity, sorrow, and wonder. India's classical dance styles have existed for more than 2,000 years. One of the oldest is the *Bharatanatyam*, which remains a popular dance. The dance is described in the *Natya Shastra*, "Treatise of Dance," which was written between 100 BCE and 300 CE. Historically, the dance was performed by a single dancer, who would move her body into different statue-like poses.

The *Dancing Girl* statue excavated in Mohenjo-Daro is one of the earliest examples of Indian dance.

CHAPTER 6

ONE LAND, MANY FAITHS

Religion has been an integral part of India's culture since its beginning. In addition to goddess figurines, the Indus seals reveal a collection of figures, including animals such as the bull, elephant, and tiger, as well as trees and gods in yoga postures. Some drawings are similar to the *linga*, a symbol of the Hindu god Shiva. Others show what appears to be Shiva with

Shiva, depicted as a modern statue in Karnataka, India, is one of the major gods of Hinduism.

65

three faces and a headdress with horns. In addition, religious figures appear in India's literature, music, and art. Today, Hinduism is the religion most commonly associated with ancient India. India's other well-known religions, Buddhism and Jainism, were reactions to Hindu beliefs.

THE ROOTS OF HINDUISM

The religion people refer to as Hinduism began more than 3,000 years ago during the Vedic era. Unlike many religions, Hinduism does not have a single founder. Rather, it developed over time, shaped from existing religious practices and beliefs.

The Indo-Aryans practiced Vedic Hinduism. The *Rigveda* is the oldest literary source related to Hinduism. The ancient Indians wrote it in approximately 300 BCE, though they shared its material orally more than 1,000 years earlier. The *Vedas* detail numerous gods—initially, 33—which these early Hindus worshiped. The deities represented elements of the natural world. Agni was the god of fire. Varuna and Vayu represented thunder and wind. Surya and Usha were the gods of sun and dawn.

The *Rigveda* features a series of poems that outline a system of sacrifice. Sacrifice was an important part of Vedic Hinduism. In *homa*, the fire-worship ritual, believers sacrificed animals, including goats, oxen, sheep, and sometimes horses. The worshipers offered their gods the meat from the sacrifices, along with bread, butter, milk, and soma, a beverage. In return, the gods supposedly granted worshipers whatever they wanted, such as long life or victory in battle.

In the 500s BCE, Brahmanism developed from Vedic Hinduism. This religion's name comes from Brahma, the almighty creator, and Brahmins, the highest caste. The idea of Brahma emerged in approximatcly 500 BCE. According to myth, Brahma came from a golden egg and created the planet Earth and everything on it. When depicted, Brahma usually has four faces, which reflect the four *Vedas* and the four social classes, among other things in Vedic Hinduism.

A page from the *Rigveda* features important Hindu hymns.

Ancient Rituals

Discoveries in the Indus Valley indicate temple rituals, ritual bathing at Mohenjo-Daro, and animal sacrifice at Kalibangan in northwest India. The Indus people followed special customs when burying their dead. They placed coffins in brick chambers with the deceased's head pointing north. Before burying a deceased person, the living would accessorize the body with ornaments. The living also provided those who died with many clay pots. The pottery varied in size, shape, and design.

The early Hindus believed in other gods as well. These deities lived in other worlds people cannot see. Eventually, Shiva, the destroyer, and Vishnu, the preserver, gained prominence when they joined Brahma in a triumvirate, or group of three. Vishnu encompasses several lesser deities as well as local heroes through avatars, or human or animal forms of gods. In approximately 500 CE, Brahma's status as a major god began to decline. Hinduism has many beliefs based on Brahmanism, including a single supreme being: God.

While Hinduism has existed for a few thousand years, the present-day version is quite different from the religion that began in ancient India. Hinduism has evolved, reflecting ideas and beliefs of the people through the ages. Upinder Singh, history professor at the University of Delhi, wrote about the complex religion:

Modern-day Hinduism differs from other major world religions in many important respects, in that it has no founder, no fixed canon which embodies its major beliefs and practices, and no organized priesthood.

It is also marked by a great variety in beliefs, practices, sects, and traditions. Some scholars argue that Hinduism is not so much a religion as a set of socio-cultural practices; others argue that it is inextricably linked to the existence of caste; and still others hold that we should talk of Hindu religions in the plural rather than the singular.[1]

BUDDHISM

By the 500s BCE, when Siddhartha Gautama lived, people were questioning Vedic Hinduism and Brahmanism, particularly sacrificial rituals. New schools of thought emerged, including Buddhism.

Om

In Hinduism, *Om* is a sacred sound. *Om* is pronounced like the word *home* without the *h*, and it has great meaning in Hindu mythology. According to Hindu belief, its vibration holds together the heavens. Om came before the universe and formed the gods. This holiest of Hindu sounds begins and ends its prayers.

The Buddha disagreed with sacrifice. He deemed the Vedic custom cruel because of the killing. He also opposed the caste system, promoting equality instead. The Buddha did not promote a god or gods. No deity would provide salvation; knowledge and meditation would.

Buddhists seek nirvana, which translates to "blowing out." Followers seek to blow out, or end, hatred, greed, and any delusions they may have. They strive for a more positive being, which will come from endless compassion, deep spirituality, and unending peace.

The Death of Buddhism in India

While Buddhism began in ancient India, it did not persist as long as it did in other regions. Followers exalted the Buddha into the realm of god, making him much more than the human being he was. Because India had so many gods, idolizing the Buddha caused him to become more ordinary. He became more myth than reality. Eventually, Buddhism receded in India, engulfed by Hinduism. However, the religion had traveled beyond India to other parts of Asia, where it thrived and continued to spread.

Buddhism experienced a great period of growth during the reign of Ashoka, from 272 BCE to 231 BCE. Ashoka converted to Buddhism and gave the religion greater recognition than it had previously. He also influenced the faith's growth, extending it beyond India. However, within a few hundred years, Buddhism greatly declined in India, although it prospered in other parts of Asia. Buddhism experienced a revival in India during the Gupta period, thanks to support from the Guptas, but then it experienced another decline that included destruction of Buddhist holy places. The first known surviving stone images of Hinduism date to the end of the Mauryan era. By the time the Guptas emerged in 320 CE, Hinduism had emerged as the most prominent religion.

JAINISM

Like Buddhism, Jainism emerged as a rejection of Vedic practices, particularly animal sacrifice. This renunciation is the religion's central belief, *ahimsa*: do no harm to any living thing.

A man named Vardhamana founded Jainism. He lived during the time of the Buddha, from 599 BCE to 527 BCE. He was also known as Mahavira. Like the Buddha, Mahavira was born of nobility and chose to give up physical comforts for a simpler life.

Jainism has three guiding principles: right belief, right conduct, and right knowledge. Each follower agrees to the five *mahavratas,* or "great vows": nonviolence, honesty, no stealing, sexual restraint, and nonattachment to possessions.

Those who practice Jainism, Jains, show their belief in nonviolence through their diet. They are strict vegetarians. In addition to practicing vegetarianism, Jains perform six rites each day. These include meditation, praying, and sitting or standing motionless for periods of time.

Jainism is highly ascetic. Mahavira lived his belief in doing no harm to any living thing. He allowed mosquitoes to feed on him and dogs to bite him. He gave up clothing because beings had to suffer in its creation. He died as a result of starving himself.

Mahavira's followers wrote down his words and memorized them to share with future followers. Jainism risked being lost because its vow of nonpossession meant its monks and nuns could not keep books, including those about their own faith. Because they were also not allowed to write, they could not record the teachings of Jainism. During the Gupta period, Jainism experienced a revival. In 460 CE, a council of Jains met and had their scriptures written down, preserving the religion.

KARMA AND TRANSMIGRATION

In the 500s BCE, as Buddhism and Jainism emerged, followers of Brahmanism advocated messages similar to those of these new faiths: asceticism, meditation, and the ancient tradition of yoga. The goal of such practices was release from the physical, material world and from *samsara*, the cycle of life, death, and transmigration, or rebirth.

Hinduism, Buddhism, and Jainism share many common beliefs. For example, all three believe in cycles, rather than in beginning and end points. The religions believe the universe is in a state of constant change, creating, preserving, and dissolving.

Karma and transmigration are two other features of all three religions. Karma is the idea that how a person lives will determine his or her life. If one thinks, says, or does good things, good fortune will come in return. But if one thinks, says, or does bad things, misfortune will result for that person. Transmigration, also called reincarnation, is the belief a person is reborn repeatedly to resolve all karmas. The soul evolves with each life.

When the soul has finished evolving, it is freed from the cycle of rebirth. Ahisma is another important part of the three faiths. It comes from the belief that all life is precious and sacred. It is closely tied to the ideas of karma and transmigration.

Other Religions

Hinduism, Buddhism, and Jainism were not the only religions in ancient India. Other practices existed. Some of them were quite different from these three faiths. For example, Goshala Maskariputra founded Ajivika at approximately the same time as Buddhism and Jainism emerged. Its name means "following the ascetic way of life," and followers of Ajivika practiced simple living rather than pursuing any particular objective. They believed in predetermination, the idea that the events of their lives were determined before birth.

The teacher Pakuda Katyayana offered another option. He preached that a person's soul is above good and evil and cannot be affected by them. The philosopher Ajita Kesakambalin encouraged materialism, believing there was no afterlife and death was the end for all souls.

CHAPTER 7

MATHEMATICS AND MEDICINE

Whole religions evolved and thrived, the minds of ancient India were also achieving great successes in mathematics. As far back as the Indus civilization, the people were skilled mathematicians. The Indus people created cities such as Harappa and Mohenjo-Daro using uniform bricks. The uniformity was mathematical, with bricks following a strict ratio

Ancient Indian architects designed cities, such as Harappa, using advanced mathematical techniques.

of 4 to 2 to 1.[1] The length was twice the size of the width, which was twice the size of the thickness.

In addition, these ancient Indians used a system of weights. Archaeologists have unearthed scales that show decimal divisions. Sizes correspond to several ratios: 0.05, 0.1, 0.2, 0.5, 1, 2, 5, 10, 20, 50, 100, 200, and 500.[2]

SKILLED AND ORIGINAL MATHEMATICIANS

The *Vedas* reveal further mathematical understanding. The people of the Vedic period understood the place value system. That is, they knew 10 is ten times greater than 1 and 100 is ten times greater than 10 and so on. The *Vedas* designate names for each place—*daza* for tens place, *zata* for hundreds place, *sahasra* for thousands place. These place designations went all the way up to the fifty-third power, or 53 zeroes.

More mathematical breakthroughs came about toward the end of the Gupta period, thanks to the work of scholar Aryabhata I. His works and life are the earliest by an Indian mathematician available

"Like the crest on the peacock's head,
Like the gem in the cobra's hood
So stands mathematics at the head of all the sciences."[3]

—*Sanskrit text* Vedanga Jyotisa, *circa 300s BCE*

to current scholars. In approximately 499 CE, he wrote about astronomy and mathematics in *Aryabhatiya* and *Aryabhatasiddhanta*, the latter of which has been lost. In *Aryabhatasiddhanta*, he treats midnight as the start of the day. He is one of the first to do so. While *Aryabhatasiddhanta* itself no longer exists, its ideas continued in later works. Among other things, Aryabhata provided formulas for determining square and cube roots. He also discussed geometry, including pi. Another of Aryabhata's achievements was calculating the length of the solar year.

MEDICINE

In addition to their mathematical advancements, the ancient Indians developed two systems of medicine: Ayurveda and Siddha. Ayurveda is a Sanskrit word that translates to "meaning of life." The *Vedas* were the first text to mention Ayurveda, which its writers believed to have come from the gods. The *Vedas* note treatments for a variety of physical ailments, including cough, diarrhea, fever, seizures, skin issues, and tumors.

Ayurveda believes five elements combine to form people: air, earth, fire, water, and ether, or space. When two or more of these elements combine, humans react in specific ways. For example, the combination of earth and water affects growth. Ayurveda also believes each person has a unique

Traditionally, medical information including Ayurveda practices
was often recorded on palm leaves.

balance of these combinations. When a person's balance is off, Ayurveda
suggests ways to restore it, including activity, diet, and massage.

Siddha originated at approximately the same time as Ayurveda and has
many similarities. The Siddha system began in southern India. Legend says
Siddha came from the Hindu god Shiva. Like Ayurveda, Siddha believes in
five elements: earth, water, fire, air, and ether.

Siddha focuses on balancing air, fire, and water, believing their imbalance causes problems. Practitioners rely on the pulse for diagnosis.

Treatment may take different paths. In Siddha, *prana*, or breathing, is the most important function of the body. Controlled breathing is intended to aid healing. *Varma* is another treatment. It involves manipulating *varmam*, points where blood vessels, bone, muscle, nerves, and tendons meet.

Like Ayurveda, Siddha looks to nature for healing through herbs. Siddha differs from Ayurveda in that it relies on combining herbs with minerals, especially mercury and sulfur. Siddha uses animal products, too. A treatment might contain an animal's blood, bones, brain, horns, liver, or skull. Practitioners also use reptile tissue in some medicines.

YOGA

Yoga is an ancient Indian tradition that is still popular today. When Siddhartha Gautama sat beneath the Bodhi tree to ponder life on his journey

The Power of Turmeric

Ayurveda advocates dozens of herbs to improve health and wellness, but turmeric is one of the most frequently mentioned. The herb is part of the ginger family and native to India. The spice is an orange-yellow color and has a distinct flavor. It is made by boiling the turmeric plant's roots and then drying them in the sun for five to seven days. Ayurveda values turmeric for its antiseptic, or germ-destroying, qualities, which are useful in treating people internally and externally. Modern practitioners still prescribe the herb for a variety of different ailments, including Alzheimer's disease, rheumatoid arthritis, and wounds.

to enlightenment, he did so in *padmasana*, a yoga pose commonly referred to as the lotus position. Yoga's existence extends well beyond the Buddha's time. It is at least as old as Mohenjo-Daro. Some of the seals discovered in the ancient city depict people in a variety of yoga positions, including padmasana.

Yoga means "union" or "yoking" in Sanskrit. It is a system of philosophy and healing that relies on the mind and body working together. The ancient Indian writer Patanjali, who lived in the 100s BCE, wrote about

According to Buddhist beliefs, Buddha sat in the lotus yoga position in his final step before becoming the Buddha, as depicted by this modern statue.

yoga in the *Yoga-sutras*. This is the earliest known literature about yoga. Previously, it had been passed down orally.

Yoga has eight stages. The second and third make up the yoga people associate with the modern practice. Asana, "seat," is a series of body positions that increase strength and flexibility. *Pranayama*, "breath control," consists of exercises that focus on breathing. The other stages focus on ethics and the mind.

While many practitioners today use yoga as simply a form of exercise, the people of ancient India sought more. By mastering yoga's stages, a practitioner would gain control of different aspects of being, which was important in obtaining spiritual goals. Siddhartha practiced yoga on his path to enlightenment.

CHAPTER 8

MILITARY MIGHT

The people of ancient India were religious and thoughtful. However, their focus on spiritual growth and understanding life and all it encompasses does not mean they were not warriors. Ancient India's history includes skilled military leaders and battles that involved tactics never before seen by enemies.

Armored elephants were a key resource used by ancient Indian warriors.

INDUS CLUES

Scholars know little about fighting during the Indus period. Writing is almost nonexistent, and researchers have not deciphered the limited script found on seals. But researchers are not without clues.

Archaeologists have unearthed a variety of weapons. Some of them could have been used for hunting. Weapons include axes, daggers, knives, maces, slings, spears, and bows and arrows. Maces had a long handle made of wood and a head made of alabaster, limestone, or sandstone. Daggers and knives were made of bronze or copper.

VEDIC FIGHTING

During the Vedic era, Indo-Aryans introduced new fighting practices to India. The group used weapons made of iron. The metal is stronger than bronze or copper.

The many kingdoms that existed during the Vedic age also put chariots to use as they fought each other. Chariots were large platforms on four wheels. Four to six horses pulled each one, which carried two to six men. Men drove the chariots

Horses

Horses were not part of life for the early Indus people. The Indo-Aryans likely brought them to India. This group valued the beasts, using them in battle, but they were important in other ways as well. Horses were a symbol of royalty. Horses also played a part in sacred practices. The Aryans identified them with the sun and sacrificed the animals in rituals.

into their enemies' armies, while archers on board showered the enemy with arrows. Other men on board had spears and protected the bowmen from attack.

In addition to spears and bows and arrows, Vedic warriors used axes, javelins, slings, and swords. The *Ramayana* and the *Mahabharata* note the *pasa* and the *sudarshana chakra*. The pasa was a noose in the shape of a triangle with iron balls that gave it weight. Soldiers used it to strangle the enemy. The sudarshana chakra was a disk with a sharp edge for throwing at opponents.

In addition to using new weapons, the Vedic people established a new organization for the military. Armies were structured into four parts: infantry, elephants, chariots, and archers. These parts were organized into intricate formations. The armies of Vedic India took to battlefields in formations with names such as the Fish, the Needle, and the Wheel. Some formations were very detailed. For example, the Lotus placed soldiers in the shape of a flower, with archers at the center, surrounded by members of the cavalry and infantry in formations like petals. The Eagle followed the shape

Chariots

The chariot was a popular vehicle in ancient times, including in ancient India. Chariots had two or four wheels. Initially, animals such as donkeys pulled the vehicles. Horses became work animals in approximately 2000 BCE, and they were faster than donkeys. A chariot pulled by a horse could reach approximately 15 miles per hour (24 kmh). Ancient Indians used chariots to hunt and for sport.

of the bird. The best troops and war elephants would form the beak and head. Fighters in chariots and on horses formed the wings. Reserve troops made up the body.

A MIGHTY MAURYAN MILITARY

When Chandragupta united the kingdoms of India into its first empire in 322 BCE, he also united their armies. He used them to build and expand the empire. The Greeks that Alexander had led onto the subcontinent

War Elephants

Elephants have been part of Indian life for millennia. The subcontinent's earliest civilization, the Indus, hunted elephants and may have tamed them. The first mention of war elephants in India is in the epic poems *Ramayana* and *Mahabharata*. Greek writings first mention ancient Indians using elephants in war in the 400s BCE. Elephants fought alongside chariots at first and eventually replaced the vehicles. A person known as a *mahout* served as an elephant's caretaker and driver. Before going into battle, the mahout would decorate the elephant's head and trunk by painting geometric shapes in bright colors on them. In 326 BCE, Alexander the Great encountered war elephants for the first time in his battle with Porus at the Hydaspes River. Alexander was impressed, saying, "I see at last a danger that matches my courage. It is at once with wild beasts and men of uncommon mettle that the contest now lies."[1] Indians used elephants in battle well beyond ancient times. India was the last nation to use war elephants, relying on the massive creatures in warfare until the 1800s CE.

had been withdrawing following the great leader's death the year before. Those who stayed joined the local culture.

The Mauryan Empire relied on people from across the land—and from all castes—to complete its military ranks. Warriors from central and western India made up the bulk of the military's soldiers. Other kingdoms provided troops only during times of war. Kingdoms in southern India provided money rather than people.

The Mauryan military continued the four-part structure of the Vedic era: infantry, elephants, chariots, and archers. The archers made up the biggest of the four groups. The military improved weaponry and armor. One improvement was a protective, miniature fortlike structure that went on the elephants' backs. From there, soldiers would attack their enemies. Weapons included bamboo bows, javelins, spears, and tridents. Elephants also carried weapons, including a sword designed for their trunks. At its largest size, the empire had

Battling Alexander

In 326 BCE, after defeating Persia, Alexander the Great set his sights on India. At the Hydaspes River, the famed Greek military leader met Porus, who ruled the Punjab region. Porus had an army of archers, chariots, elephants, and infantry. The archers used bamboo bows that were six feet (2 m) long and long arrows made of cane.[2] The mighty elephants wore bronze masks and were a new challenge for the Greeks, but Porus and his army were no match for Alexander and his superior military leadership. Porus's infantry sought protection by huddling near the elephants, but the beasts were wounded and angry and trampled people nearby. Those not crushed were left to face Alexander's cavalry, which overpowered them.

750,000 soldiers and more than 9,000 elephants.[3]

GUPTA POWER

The end of the Mauryan Empire led to a fractured India. Kingdoms fought one another, as well as invaders from outside. Ancient India had no single organized military, until the rise of the Gupta Empire in the 300s CE.

The military of the Gupta Empire was similar to those of previous eras. It had four parts. However, instead of chariots, it relied on a cavalry. The military armed these foot soldiers with lances or swords. Archers remained an important part of the Gupta military. Their strength was improved by an advancement in bow design. Warriors from the upper castes had bows made of steel. They were stronger than

Shields provided additional protection for ancient Indian warriors. They varied in shape and decoration.

bamboo bows. With them, an archer could shoot farther and puncture thick armor. Unlike bamboo, steel would not warp in the humidity of some regions of the subcontinent. However, archers of the lower castes still used bamboo longbows. Most used bamboo arrows, which were often set on fire before shooting. Other fighting instruments included daggers and swords.

"The Persians are famed for their archers, the Turks for their horsemen, and India for its armies."[5]

—Arab proverb

Soldiers from the upper castes and the best fighters had other, better equipment, including steel weapons such as broadswords. They had chain mail, too, but it was challenging to wear in the hot environment of India.

Just like the mighty Mauryan military at its peak, the Gupta Empire had 750,000 soldiers.[4] Tools such as the catapult gave them an even greater advantage over their enemies. And the expansion of the empire proves the Gupta military's knowledge of battle techniques.

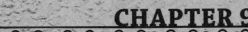

CHAPTER 9

ANCIENT INDIA'S LEGACY

The end of the Gupta Empire in 550 CE marked the end of the ancient period of India's history. The following centuries would continue to bring changes, including rule by Middle Eastern nations and Europeans. However, time and outside influences did not diminish the culture that had developed on the subcontinent through great periods such as the Indus,

Many of the aspects of ancient India, including religion, art, and architecture, have carried through into modern Indian culture.

Vedic, Mauryan, and Gupta. Rather, these changes simply added to India's rich culture and history.

THE MAKING OF MODERN INDIA

The generations following India's golden age saw leaders come and go. The 700s CE brought the first of many Middle Eastern invaders. Later, a string of Muslim empires known as the Delhi Sultanate controlled much of northern India from 1206 to 1526.

The Mughal Empire (1526–1858) followed. Its rulers were descended from the Mongols. The era was relatively peaceful, and culture thrived. One of India's landmarks, the Taj Mahal, was born during this era. The emperor, Shah Jahan, built it in Agra as a mausoleum for his wife. Construction took almost 20 years.

All the while, trade continued between India and other countries. Portuguese traders arrived by sea in India at the end of the 1400s. Other Europeans followed in the 1600s, including the Dutch, French, and British. The British arrival in particular would have a lasting effect on India.

During the British rule of India, battles frequently broke out between the native Indians and the British colonists.

The British East India Company came to India in 1608. Its owners were interested in goods such as jewels, silk, and spices. Labor was inexpensive, which encouraged expansion. The company set up factories.

The Caste System Today

The caste system continues to divide India's people today. The names of the four main classes have not changed, though some of their areas of work reflect modernity. Brahmins focus on scriptural education and teaching. Kshatriyas are dedicated to public service. The Vaishya form a business caste. The Shudra caste consists of semiskilled and unskilled workers. Untouchables make up a fifth class, which consists of people considered the lowest of society. Today, the castes mingle in business and social situations. However, people rarely marry outside their caste, and a person cannot change his or her caste.

It grew and became successful and powerful, bit by bit, taking over the country. Eventually, the company used force to fight local people who revolted against it. The British government tried to control the company and ultimately disbanded it in 1858, installing a colonial government on the subcontinent.

Direct rule by the British is known as the British Raj. It began in 1858. During that time, the British imposed their customs on Indian society, including the English language. Tea was a major crop, with India providing 59 percent of Britain's supply. However, as the British prospered from exporting tea, the Indian people continued suffering. The poor remained poor, while the British living in India grew richer.

Independence movements began forming in the late 1800s. Finally, in 1947, India gained independence. In the process, it lost part of its northwest territory, which became part of Pakistan.

On January 26, 1950, India became a republic. After centuries of foreign rule, India was independent.

Since gaining its independence, India has warred with Pakistan. Other issues facing the nation have included overpopulation and poverty. However, the country has experienced tremendous economic growth in recent decades, too, becoming a power regionally and globally.

RELIGIOUS CONTRIBUTIONS

Ancient India's contributions are apparent in India and abroad, and its influence on world religion is undeniable. The Hindu, Buddhist, and Jain belief systems that started so long ago continue. Hinduism is the third-largest religion in the world, with almost 1 billion followers, mostly in South Asia.[2] Almost 81 percent of Indians are Hindu.[3]

Almost 6 percent of the world's population practices Buddhism. Most Buddhists are in Southeast Asia, but the belief system's following outside Asia is growing. Many people in Australia, Europe, North America, and South America follow the teachings of the Buddha.

Jainism has more than 4.5 million followers.[4] Most of them are in India, but Jains also live in Africa, Europe, and North America.

The ancient practice of yoga is thriving in the United States and other parts of the world.

OLD PRACTICES IN A NEW ERA

India has a short history as a nation and a long history as a people. The Indian culture has continuity unlike any other. It is rich in tradition, religion, artistry, and knowledge, reflecting and building on its impressive and important past. The influence of the Indo-Aryans lives on daily for millions of modern Indians who practice Hinduism. But India's history lives on in other ways. Yoga exists beyond India's borders. And while the West has its own forms of medicine, Westerners are embracing holistic ideas such as those presented by Ayurveda. In addition, mathematical concepts used in ancient India, such as pi, are alive and well.

India does not simply have a history, it is history. Those who inhabit the subcontinent live that history daily. They shape it and add to it, just as their ancestors did. As the young nation of India moves forward, it does so with an eye toward its past, its people well aware of themselves as a culture millennia old, adept, aware, artistic, and worthy of awe. Its rich, complex story continues to unfold.

Art and Architecture

Very few people yet realize how great a debt the art of the world—especially that of the Eastern world—owes to India. It is true to say that without the example of Indian forms and ideas, the arts of the whole of South East Asia, of China, Korea, Mongolia, Tibet, and Japan would all have been radically different. . . . So, too, would modern Western art, especially architecture and painting.[5]

—P. S. Rawson, art historian

TIMELINE

3300 BCE–1700 BCE
The Indus civilization flourishes in northern and central India.

1700 BCE–500 BCE
The Vedic civilization is prominent.

1500 BCE
The Aryans arrive in India.

600 BCE
Sixteen *mahajanapadas*, "great kingdoms," emerge.

500s BCE
The founders of Jainism and Buddhism are born.

400 BCE
The *Mahabharata*, the world's longest poem, is written down.

327 BCE
Alexander the Great becomes the first Greek to invade India.

321 BCE
Chandragupta Maurya unites India's kingdoms into its first empire.

C. 273 BCE–232 BCE
Ashoka leads the Mauryan Empire, spreading his Buddhist beliefs in a collection of edicts.

185 BCE
The Mauryan dynasty ends.

100s BCE

Artists create the first five caves at Ajanta, which serve as temples.

C. 100 BCE–300 CE

The *Natya Shastra*, "Treatise of Dance," is completed.

320

The Gupta Empire begins, marking the start of India's golden age, a time of great artistic expression and advances in mathematics and medicine.

C. 400

The *Dattilam* details a system for Indian music.

400s

Kalidasa writes the *Abhijnanashakuntala*, India's best literary work.

400s AND 500s

Artists create additional caves at Ajanta, creating what becomes classical Indian art.

499

Aryabhata I writes about mathematics and astronomy in *Aryabhatiya*.

550

The Gupta Empire ends, marking the end of India's golden age.

ANCIENT HISTORY

KEY DATES

- 3300 BCE: The Indus civilization settled in northern and central India, existing until 1700 BCE.

- 1700 BCE: The Vedic civilization begins, lasting until 500 BCE.

- 500s BCE: The founders of Jainism and Buddhism were born.

- 321 BCE–185 BCE: India's first empire, the Mauryan Empire, existed.

- 320 CE–550 CE: The Gupta Empire created India's golden age, a time of great artistic expression and advances in mathematics and medicine.

KEY TOOLS AND TECHNOLOGIES

- The Indus civilization created the first water and sewer systems.

- Ancient Indian warriors improved bow and arrow technology, giving them some of the best archers in the ancient world.

- Ancient Indians built Indus cities, including Harappa and Mohenjo-Daro, using uniform bricks.

LANGUAGE

Sanskrit, which is still spoken today, was the predominant language in ancient India. It is part of the Indo-European languages group, which also contains Greek and Latin.

IMPACT OF THE INDIAN CIVILIZATION

- Literature and religion highlight ancient India's culture, with the *Vedas* providing important clues to Hinduism's past. Parts of the ancient texts, such as the *Bhagavad Gita*, remain important material to Hindus.

- Hinduism, Buddhism, and Jainism began on the subcontinent long ago and are practiced there still today, as well as in lands near and far.

- Religion and art combined in the Ajanta caves to create art that remains as evidence of India's golden age. The style ancient Indian artists created is visible today in other Asian countries.

QUOTE

"Every generation in India, for over 4,000 years, has bequeathed something, if only a very little to posterity. No land on earth has such a long cultural continuity as India. . . . In India, the brahman still repeats in his daily worship Vedic hymns composed over 3,000 years ago, and tradition recalls heroic chieftains and the great battles fought by them at about the same time. In respect of the length of continuous tradition, China comes second to India and Greece makes a poor third."

—*A. L. Basham, a historian specializing in South Asia*, The Illustrated Cultural History of India

GLOSSARY

avatar
In Hinduism, the human or animal form a deity takes to fight an evil on earth.

Brahma
In Hinduism, the creator god.

Buddhism
The religion based on the teachings of the Buddha, who advocated pursuing a middle path in life, avoiding the extremes of indulgence and self-denial.

dharma
In Hinduism, religious or moral law that varies with caste; in Buddhism, the truth of the universe that exists for all people always, particularly, the ideas of karma and rebirth; in Jainism, moral virtue.

dynasty
A family that controls a country for a long period of time through successive rulers.

edict
A declaration or order by someone in power.

ghee
Butter prepared using a process of heating and cooling that results in it being semifluid.

Hinduism
The main religion in India; it involves worshiping numerous gods and stresses karma and reincarnation.

Jainism
A disciplined religion that stresses nonviolence; depending on the worshiper, this could be animals or all living things.

karma
The force that results from a person's thoughts or actions and determines what a person's current or next life will be like.

patriarchal
Passed down through the male line.

soapstone
A kind of stone that is soft and feels like soap.

stupa
A moundlike structure that is a Buddhist shrine, often containing a relic of the Buddha or identifying a sacred location.

Vedas
The earliest sacred writings of Hinduism.

ADDITIONAL RESOURCES

SELECTED BIBLIOGRAPHY

Avari, Burjor. *India: The Ancient Past: A History of the Indian Subcontinent from c. 7000 to AD 1200.* New York: Routledge, 2007. Print.

Basham, A. L., ed. *The Illustrated Cultural History of India.* New York: Oxford UP, 2007. Print.

Chandra, Anjana Motihar. *India Condensed: 5,000 Years of History and Culture.* Singapore: Marshall Cavendish, 2008. Print.

FURTHER READINGS

Albanese, Marilia. *India: Treasures from an Ancient World.* Vercilli, Italy: White Star, 2001. Print.

Ali, Daud. *Ancient India: Discover the Rich Heritage of the Indus Valley and the Mughal Empire, with 15 Step-by-Step Projects and 340 Pictures.* West Chester, PA: Armadillo, 2014. Print.

Dalal, Anita. *Ancient India: Archaeology Unlocks the Secrets of India's Past.* Washington, DC: National Geographic Children's, 2007. Print.

WEBSITES

To learn more about Ancient Civilizations, visit **booklinks.abdopublishing.com**. These links are routinely monitored and updated to provide the most current information available.

PLACES TO VISIT
THE BRITISH MUSEUM

Great Russell Street

London WC1B 3DG, United Kingdom

+44 (0)20 7323 8299

http://www.britishmuseum.org/explore/cultures/asia/ancient_south_asia.aspx

Room 33 contains objects from India's ancient past, including some from Buddhism, Hinduism, and Jainism.

NATIONAL MUSEUM, NEW DELHI

Janpath and Rajpath Roads

New Delhi, India

011-23792775

http://www.nationalmuseumindia.gov.in/visiting.asp

Collections include the Indus civilization, Buddhist art, and archaeology, the last of which includes 800 sculptures dating from the third century BCE.

SOURCE NOTES

Chapter 1. The Birth of Buddhism

1. "Seeking." *The Buddha*. PBS, David Grubin Productions, 2010. Web. 23 June 2014.

2. "Death & Legacy." *The Buddha*. PBS, David Grubin Productions, 2010. Web. 23 June 2014.

3. John Bowker, ed. *The Cambridge Illustrated History of Religions*. Cambridge, UK: Cambridge UP, 2002. Print. 79.

4. "Birth & Youth." *The Buddha*. PBS, David Grubin Productions, 2010. Web. 10 Sept. 2014.

Chapter 2. Settling the Subcontinent

1. "Harappa." *History Today*. History Today Ltd., 2012. Web. 10 Sept. 2014.

2. Anjana Motihar Chandra. *India Condensed: 5000 Years of History and Culture*. Singapore: Marshall Cavendish, 2009. Print. 21.

3. Encyclopædia Britannica. "Indus Civilization." *Encyclopædia Britannica*. Encyclopædia Britannica, 12 Mar. 2014. Web. 20 May 2014.

4. Time-Life Books. *Ancient India: Land of Mystery*. Alexandria, VA: Time-Life, 1994. Print. 21–25.

5. Burjor Avari. *India: The Ancient Past: A History of the Indian Subcontinent from c. 7000 BC to AD 1200*. New York: Routledge, 2007. Print. 43–44.

Chapter 3. Chiefs, Kings, and Castes

1. Amulya Chandra Sen. "Ashoka." *Encyclopædia Britannica*. Encyclopædia Britannica, 2 Jan. 2014. Web. 26 May 2014.

Chapter 4. Life Based in Faith

1. Aleem Maqbool. "Mohenjo Daro: Could This Ancient City Be Lost Forever?" *BBC News*. BBC, 26 June 2012. Web. 22 July 2014.
2. Ibid.

Chapter 5. Literature, Art, Music, and Dance

1. Sanujit. "Initiation of Religions in India." *Ancient History Encyclopedia*. Ancient History Encyclopedia Limited, 23 July 2011. Web. 21 June 2014.
2. Time-Life Books. *Ancient India: Land of Mystery*. Alexandria, VA: Time-Life, 1994. Print. 57.
3. "History of Haryana: Mahabharat War, 900 BC Approximately." *Mahabharat*. Haryana Online, 2009. Web. 10 Sept. 2014.
4. A. L. Basham, ed. *The Illustrated Cultural History of India*. New York: Oxford UP, 2007. Print. 73.

SOURCE NOTES CONTINUED

Chapter 6. One Land, Many Faiths

1. Upinder Singh. *A History of Ancient and Early Medieval India: From the Stone Age to the 12th Century.* New Delhi, India: Dorling Kindersley, 2008. Print. 433.

Chapter 7. Mathematics and Medicine

1. Burjor Avarir. *India: The Ancient Past: A History of the Indian Subcontinent from c. 7000 BC to AD 1200.* New York: Routledge, 2007. Print.

2. Anjana Motihar Chandra. *India Condensed: 5000 Years of History and Culture.* Singapore: Marshall Cavendish, 2009. Print. 133.

3. "Math, Science, and Technology in India: From the Ancient to the Recent." *Asia Society.* Asia Society, 2014. Web. 10 Sept. 2014.

Chapter 8. Military Might

1. Konstantin Nossov. *War Elephants*. Lincoln: U of Nebraska P, 2008. Print. 32.

2. "The Military of Ancient India." *AncientMilitary.com*. AncientMilitary.com, 2012. Web. 15 June 2014.

3. Ibid.

4. Ibid.

5. "Military History of Ancient India." *All Empires*. All Empires, 2006. Web. 10 Sept. 2014.

Chapter 9. Ancient India's Legacy

1. Joanne O'Brien and Martin Palmer. *The Atlas of Religion*. Berkeley, CA: U of California P, 2007. 27.

2. "India." *The World Factbook*. Central Intelligence Agency, 22 June 2014. Web. 23 June 2014.

3. Joanne O'Brien and Martin Palmer. *The Atlas of Religion*. Berkeley, CA: U of California P, 2007. 26.

4. A. L. Basham, ed. *The Illustrated Cultural History of India*. New York: Oxford UP, 2007. Print. 2–3.

5. Ibid. 119.

INDEX

ABOUT THE AUTHOR

Rebecca Rowell has worked on numerous books for young readers as an author and as an editor. Her writing includes titles about the social media, the US Marine Corps, pop singer and songwriter Pink, education advocate Malala Yousafzai, and Switzerland. One of her favorite parts of writing is doing research and learning about all kinds of subjects. Rebecca has a master's degree in publishing and writing from Emerson College. She currently lives in Minneapolis, Minnesota.